OREGON

ALASKA

CANADA

PACIFIC
OCEAN

UNITED
STATES

HAWAII

PUERTO
RICO

MEXICO

OREGON

HELLO
U.S.A.

by Gretchen Bratvold

Lerner Publications Company

You'll find this picture of an Oregon grape plant at the beginning of each chapter in this book. This plant's small yellow flowers bloom in early summer. Its dark berries become ripe in late fall and can be used in cooking. The flower of the Oregon grape plant was chosen as Oregon's state flower in 1899.

Cover (left): Downtown Portland. Cover (right): Cut lumber from an Oregon forest. Pages 2–3: Tourists at Bullards Beach State Park. Page 3: Willamette National Forest.

This book is available in two editions:
Library binding by Lerner Publications Company, a division of Lerner Publishing Group
Soft cover by First Avenue Editions, an imprint of Lerner Publishing Group
241 First Avenue North
Minneapolis, MN 55401 U.S.A.

Website address: www.lernerbooks.com

Library of Congress Cataloging-in-Publication Data

Bratvold, Gretchen, 1959–
      Oregon / by Gretchen Bratvold — Rev. and expanded.
         p.   cm. — (Hello U.S.A.)
      Includes index.
      Summary: An introduction to Oregon and its geography, history, people, and economy.
      ISBN 0–8225–4099–1 (lib. bdg. : alk. paper)
      ISBN 0–8225–0792–7 (pbk. : alk. paper)
      1. Oregon—Juvenile literature. [1. Oregon.] I. Title. II. Series.
      F876.3 .B73   2003
      979.5—dc21   2002004512

Manufactured in the United States of America
1 2 3 4 5 6 – JR – 08 07 06 05 04 03

CONTENTS

Many of the mountains in the Cascades—including Mount Hood—are volcanoes, but they have not erupted for centuries.

THE LAND

Mountains to Coast

ometimes called the Pacific Wonderland, Oregon is located on the Pacific coast of the northwestern United States. It is part of the region known as the Pacific Northwest.

Mountains, sand dunes, and misty shores make Oregon an outdoor paradise. Washington, Idaho, Nevada, and California border the state on three sides. The Pacific Ocean washes against Oregon's western shore.

Millions of years ago, shallow seas covered part of what later became Oregon and the land was much flatter. Gradually, the seas dried up and the earth's crust began to shift, pushing up mountains along the western coast.

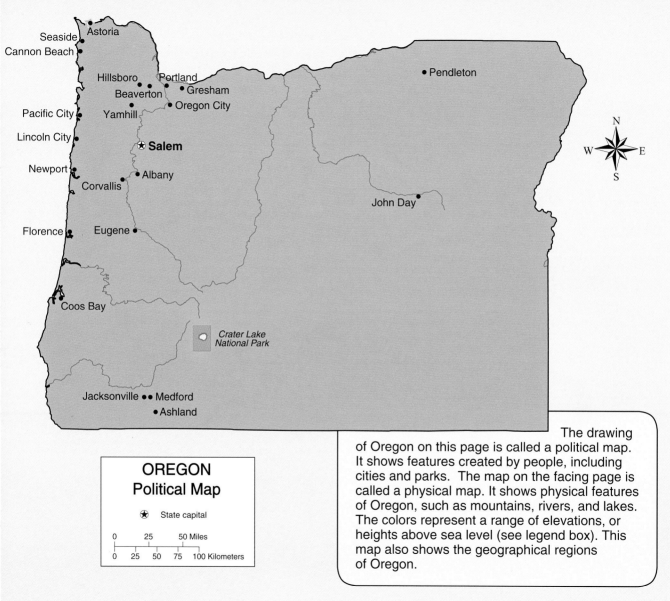

Seaside
Astoria
Cannon Beach
Hillsboro   Portland
Beaverton   ● Gresham
Pacific City   Yamhill   ● Oregon City
Lincoln City
★ **Salem**
Newport
Albany
Corvallis
Florence   Eugene

● Pendleton

John Day

Coos Bay

Crater Lake
National Park

Jacksonville ● ● Medford
● Ashland

N
W   E
S

OREGON
Political Map

(★) State capital

0   25   50 Miles

0   25   50   75   100 Kilometers

The drawing of Oregon on this page is called a political map. It shows features created by people, including cities and parks. The map on the facing page is called a physical map. It shows physical features of Oregon, such as mountains, rivers, and lakes. The colors represent a range of elevations, or heights above sea level (see legend box). This map also shows the geographical regions of Oregon.

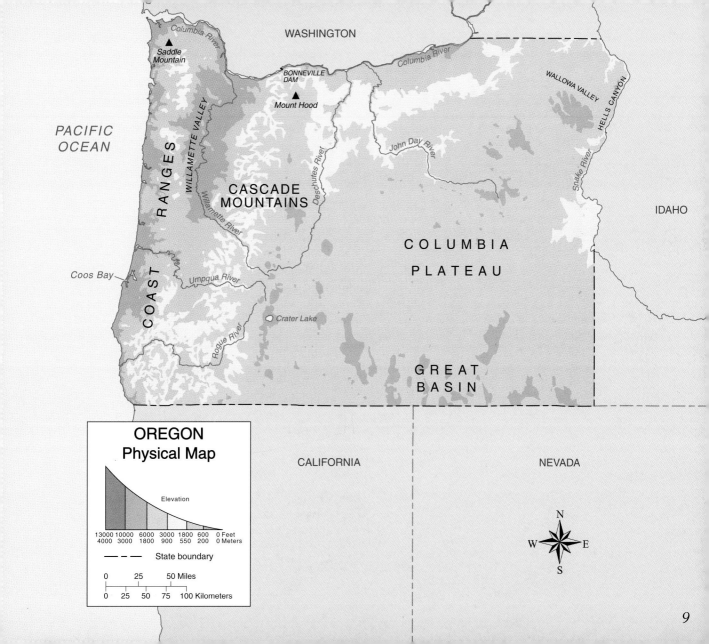

WASHINGTON

Columbia River

▲
Saddle
Mountain

PACIFIC
OCEAN

BONNEVILLE
DAM

Columbia River

WALLOWA VALLEY

▲
Mount Hood

HELLS CANYON

Deschutes River

John Day River

Snake River

IDAHO

CASCADE
MOUNTAINS

COLUMBIA

PLATEAU

C O A S T R A N G E S

WILLAMETTE VALLEY

Willamette River

Coos Bay

Umpqua River

○ Crater Lake

Rogue River

G R E A T
B A S I N

CALIFORNIA

NEVADA

OREGON
Physical Map

Elevation

| 13000 | 10000 | 6000 | 3000 | 1800 | 600 | 0 Feet |
| 4000 | 3000 | 1800 | 900 | 550 | 200 | 0 Meters |

– – – State boundary

| 0 | 25 | 50 Miles |

| 0 | 25 | 50 | 75 | 100 Kilometers |

N
W   E
S

Visitors at Lava Lands in central Oregon can explore a moonlike landscape shaped by volcanoes.

Oregon's Cascade Mountains began deep underground. Gases and molten rock began to bubble up to the earth's surface, and volcanoes erupted. They spouted ash and **lava,** melted rock that hardens into solid rock as it cools.

Over time, the lava and ash built up higher and higher around the mouths of the volcanoes, eventually forming the Cascade Mountains. Lava also gushed from cracks in the earth's crust and flowed across broad expanses, hardening into layers of rock that later became thousands of feet thick. Oregon's Columbia Plateau, a highland region, was formed this way.

Mountain ranges cover most of the state. The Coast Ranges stretch along the western part of Oregon. These mountains are the lowest in the state. Along much of the shore, steep cliffs rise sharply from the ocean. Inland, the northern half of the Coast Ranges flatten out into the valley of the Willamette River. This small but fertile area is home to more than half of Oregon's people.

East of the Coast Ranges, the Cascade Mountains divide western Oregon from eastern Oregon. The highest mountains in the state, the Cascades contain several peaks that rise over 10,000 feet.

One of the highest peaks in the Coast Ranges, Saddle Mountain offers a good view of the surrounding area.

The Columbia Plateau fills most of eastern Oregon. Although **plateaus** are usually flat highlands, mountains cover much of this region, especially in the northeast. Streams have cut deep **canyons** into the thick volcanic rock that forms the plateau. Most of the people who live here grow wheat, Oregon's most valuable crop.

At Smith Rock State Park on the Columbia Plateau, walls of sheer rock challenge climbers.

The desert areas of the Great Basin are alive with rich colors in the fall.

South of the Columbia Plateau is a region called the Great Basin. Mountains and valleys extend across this region. Some of the Great Basin is so dry that it is considered **desert.** That means that less than 10 inches of rain fall per year. Water from the region's few streams dries up before it can flow out to the ocean.

Hundreds of rivers and streams drain rain and snow from Oregon's Cascade and Coast Mountains. The Columbia River, Oregon's biggest, is 7 miles wide where it enters the Pacific Ocean. Large, oceangoing ships can travel 200 miles up the waterway before it becomes too shallow. The Willamette, Deschutes, and Snake Rivers flow into the Columbia.

The Columbia and the Snake Rivers have carved deep canyons through the Columbia Plateau. Hells Canyon, along the Snake River, averages a depth of 5,500 feet. Several other rivers—including the Rogue and Umpqua—flow from the Cascades into the Pacific.

Many small lakes dot the slopes of the Cascade Mountains. Crater Lake, the deepest lake in the United States, sits within the collapsed walls of Mount Mazama, an extinct volcano.

Oregon has two different climates—one west of the Cascade Mountains and another east of this barrier. To the west, temperatures change little throughout the year. This area receives a lot of rain—sometimes over 130 inches in a year.

Crater Lake's ice-cold waters descend to a depth of 1,932 feet.

When rain clouds move in from the ocean, they must rise to pass over the mountains. As the clouds rise, they drop their moisture on the Coast Ranges and the western slopes of the Cascades. By the time the clouds cross the Cascades, they have lost almost all of their moisture, making the eastern side of the state very dry. Here, temperatures dip below freezing in the winter and average 72° F in the summer.

Forests of cedar, fir, pine, ash, and maple cover much of western Oregon. But only a few hardy trees can survive in the dry climate east of the Cascades. Grasses and sagebrush are the main plants that grow in this eastern region.

The Indian paintbrush brightens Oregon's countryside with its colorful petals.

Eastern Oregon is home to pronghorn antelope, which feed on the region's grasses and shrubs.

Oregon's wildlife also varies from one side of the Cascades to the other. Elk and deer feed on the lush vegetation of western Oregon. In the east, bighorn sheep and pronghorn antelope climb the rocky slopes. The state is famous for its salmon, which swim from the ocean up Oregon's rivers each spring to lay their eggs. Seals and sea lions feast on fish and squid along the coast.

Following the Trail

The lush forests of western Oregon provided abundant wildlife for early Indian hunters.

The first humans in the Oregon area arrived more than 12,000 years ago. These people were American Indians, or Native Americans. They lived at a place later called Fort Rock Caves. Signs of human life at Fort Rock vanished after 5000 B.C., when Mount Mazama erupted. But **archaeologists** have uncovered some clues to this distant past. Among their finds are stone tools and sandals made from sagebrush bark.

Other Indians lived along the Columbia River, where they caught and dried enough salmon each spring to last the whole year. The people held a huge thanksgiving ceremony to celebrate the first catch of the year. At this feast, they sampled the fish and returned its skeleton to the river.

Many early Oregonians made their homes along the Columbia River.

Little else is known about American Indian life in the Oregon area before the 1700s, when European explorers arrived in the region. From the explorers we know that several groups of Indians lived in the area at that time. Most of them lived along the coast, where the ocean and thick forests offered plenty of fish and game for food.

Coastal Indians such as the Chinook and the Tillamook were experienced traders, often using

Flattened foreheads were considered a sign of beauty by Chinook Indians. To achieve this look, mothers strapped their infants in a cradleboard. The device had a hinged board that clamped down to shape the head into a straight line from the crown to the tip of the nose.

seashells for money. Sometimes they traded with Indians from the Cascade Mountains and the Columbia Plateau.

Native Americans from these eastern regions included the Modoc, Klamath, Nez Perce, and Cayuse. Because most of the area was dry, these Indians lived in villages along rivers. In the spring they caught salmon, and they also dug wild roots for food. During the 1700s, the Nez Perce and Cayuse became skilled horse riders and breeders.

Few Indians lived in the dry Great Basin region to the south, where food was scarce. Those who did live in the area spent much of their time looking for food—nuts, berries, roots, snakes, lizards, insects. Finding enough water and firewood was also a constant challenge. The Paiute and other Indians in this region wove beautiful baskets from grasses that grew there.

These portable homes, called longhouses, were used by Indians along the Columbia River. Made by weaving grass mats to cover a frame of wooden poles, the shelters could house several people.

Fur from sea otters brought huge profits for fur traders. By the late 1800s, hardly any of the animals were left.

The first Europeans to stumble upon Oregon's Indians probably came from Great Britain. The British took an interest in the Pacific Northwest in the late 1700s. The explorers James Cook and George Vancouver both thought the region would be ideal for fur trading.

Cook befriended the Chinook. Expert trappers and traders, these Indians exchanged furs from seals and sea otters for knives, nails, buttons, and blankets.

Cook's crew discovered they could make a fortune selling the valuable furs. In Asia, where furs were very popular, the animal skins sold for as much as $100 each.

Word of the profits to be made selling furs from the Pacific Northwest spread to others. Americans from the newly formed United States (on the eastern side of the continent) also took an interest in the region.

In 1792 Robert Gray, an American, sailed along the coast of the Pacific Northwest. Here, he found a thunderous river and named it after his ship, the *Columbia.*

Exploration of the Columbia River by Robert Gray strengthened U.S. claims to the region.

In 1805 two other American adventurers, Meriwether Lewis and William Clark, reached Oregon the hard way—by land. Lewis and Clark had explored western North America in search of the best land route across the continent to the Pacific Ocean.

After nearly 18 months of travel, Lewis and Clark finally reached the Columbia River. They then followed the river to the Pacific Ocean.

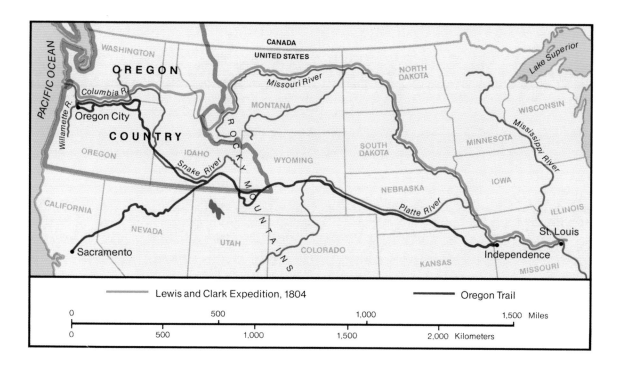

Lewis and Clark Expedition, 1804

Oregon Trail

| 0 | 500 | 1,000 | 1,500 Miles |

| 0 | 500 | 1,000 | 1,500 | 2,000 Kilometers |

They had traveled 2,000 miles—all the way from Missouri—forging part of the route that became known as the Oregon Trail. At the entrance to the Columbia River, members of the expedition built their winter quarters, which they called Fort Clatsop. The expedition headed back to Missouri in March 1806. Their work helped strengthen the U.S. claim on the region.

Both Britain and the United States claimed the Oregon Country—a huge area between California and Alaska and between the Pacific Ocean and the Rocky Mountains. In the early 1800s, both British and American pioneers began to settle in the region.

In 1821 the British asked a man named John McLoughlin to start a fur-trading operation in the Pacific Northwest for the Hudson's Bay Company. In 1825 McLoughlin opened Fort Vancouver (in what later became the state of Washington) near the mouth of the Willamette River. McLoughlin gave plots of land to people who worked for the Hudson's Bay Company—an action that encouraged more British people to settle in the region. At the same time, American **missionaries** (Christians who wanted to spread their religion among the Indians) slowly began to arrive in the Pacific Northwest.

Other Americans began to hear stories about Oregon's rich soil. In 1843 about 1,000 people arrived in the first wagon train to travel the Oregon Trail. Most of these **immigrants** (newcomers) chose to farm the fertile Willamette Valley.

Immigrants pause to eat, rest, and play at a camp along the Oregon Trail.

As more Americans settled in the Willamette Valley, Britain and the United States agreed to split the Oregon Country between them. In 1846 the United States took the southern part, where most of the Americans were living, and Britain took the northern portion, in what later became Canada.

Within two years of the arrival of the first wagon train, Oregon City had grown into a thriving town.

Settlers traveled to Oregon by wagon train or on foot. The flood of newcomers lasted nearly 100 years.

By 1859, Americans in Oregon had set up a government, and Oregon became the 33rd state to join the Union.

Immigrants continued to come to Oregon, and the Indians in the area began to distrust the white settlers. Wagon trains scared away game, and the newcomers settled on Indian territory. Thousands of Indians died from diseases brought into the region by the immigrants. Indian attacks became common as more settlers arrived.

Chief Joseph of the Nez Perce

The U.S. government forced chiefs of Indian tribes, including the Nez Perce, to sign **treaties.** By signing these agreements, the Native Americans gave up claims to much of their territory. In exchange, the United States gave the Indians a piece of land on which they were told they could live undisturbed. This land was to be their **reservation.**

Often, the U.S. government did not live up to the terms of the treaties. Different tribes were placed on the same reservation. Sometimes the tribes that were put together had been longtime enemies.

Oregon's Indians had traditionally hunted and gathered their food. But on the reservations, government agents forced them to farm crops. The government broke many of its promises to provide education, supplies, and money to the Indians.

The Nez Perce War

The Nez Perce at one time proudly claimed that they had never killed a white person. But in the 1860s, gold brought eager white settlers to the Nez Perce reservation. The U.S. government told those Nez Perce who lived in the Wallowa Valley in northeastern Oregon to move to another reservation in Idaho. Some Indians refused to leave.

More white settlers came in 1873, this time to herd cattle. Chief Joseph, leader of the Wallowa group of Nez Perce, did not want to fight, but he also wanted to stay on the land where his parents were buried. He remembered the words of his dying father: "Never sell the bones of your father and your mother."

In 1877 a group of young Nez Perce warriors killed several white people. The whites wanted revenge, and Joseph's people had no choice left but to fight. Joseph had only 200 warriors and another 400 women, children, and older people. The settlers had an entire army—hundreds of soldiers ready to defeat the Nez Perce. Yet, battle after battle, the Nez Perce crushed the heavily armed U.S. troops.

But Joseph knew his people could not win every fight and that their only hope was to escape. For four months they traveled over deserts and mountains, heading toward Canada, where the army would not follow them. The trek was difficult, and food and other supplies often ran low. As winter approached, the Indians grew very tired.

Just 30 miles from the Canadian border, the U.S. Army caught up to the Nez Perce and surrounded their camp. Chief Joseph knew the end had come. He got on his horse and slowly rode up to the U.S. general.

"I am tired of fighting," Joseph said. "Our chiefs are killed. . . . It is cold and we have no blankets, no food. The little children are freezing to death. . . . My heart is sick and sad. From where the sun now stands, I will fight no more forever."

After a 1,700-mile journey, Joseph's surrender speech captured the feelings of all his people. The leader of the Nez Perce was never permitted to return to his homeland. When Joseph died in 1904, his doctor reported that he had died of a broken heart.

By 1888 Portland's population had reached 60,000. It surpassed Oregon City as the largest community in the Pacific Northwest.

Between 1860 and 1890, thousands of people moved to Oregon from the midwestern United States and from northern Europe. As farmland in the Willamette Valley filled up, immigrants tried their luck at mining or farming on the Columbia Plateau.

Other newcomers chopped down trees or worked at factories in Portland, which had grown to be Oregon's largest city. When the Northern Pacific Railroad opened in 1883, Oregonians began sending lumber and other goods to the eastern coast of the United States at record speeds.

Asians came from China and Japan to work on railroads or in mines. They were so eager to get jobs that they worked for very low wages. Many Oregonians disliked the Asians simply because they were different. Some Oregonians kept Asians from voting or owning land.

The building of railroads in Oregon allowed factories to ship more products to the East Coast.

Oregon's laws were not kind to everyone. But compared to other states, Oregon was considered a leader in setting up a fair system of government. The state passed laws that allowed most of its people to participate more directly in the government. They had more control over what became law, and they could vote people out of office.

During the 1930s, Oregonians built Bonneville Dam on the Columbia River. The water that surged through the dam turned huge engines, which created electricity.

Working high above the Columbia River, workers constructed Bonneville Dam in the mid-1930s.

Canned salmon was among the first goods manufactured in Oregon.

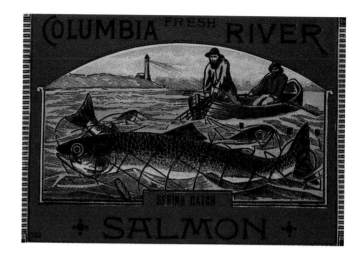

This form of energy—called **hydropower**—provided inexpensive electrical power needed to run machines at many factories. The dam also controlled the level of the river's water, which made it easier for ships to travel.

More dams were built in the 1950s and 1960s. With the growth of hydropower, more industries came to Oregon to take advantage of the cheap source of energy. In the fields, farmers started using more efficient machinery for some of their chores, so they didn't need as many helping hands. The extra people moved from the country to cities, where they took up work in factories.

Soil in the dry, eastern part of Oregon is excellent for growing wheat, the state's most important crop. The rise of irrigation in the mid-1900s allowed farmers to grow more crops.

The new dams provided water for **irrigation** as well as energy for electricity. By irrigating, farmers could channel water from the rivers to their fields. Even areas that did not get much rain could get enough water for farming. As machinery and irrigation of farms increased, so did the size of harvests. Many crops were sent to be canned at food processing plants in cities.

During this period, lumbering grew into a major business. The state's thick forests provided millions of trees—enough to construct more than half of the new homes built in the United States each year. Until the 1960s, sawdust, bark, and other lumber scraps were thrown away. Then people began finding new uses for these materials. They were saved and reused to make new wood products, such as hardboard, chipboard, and particleboard.

While the lumber industry was growing, some people wanted to protect Oregon's forests from overcutting. New trees could not be planted fast enough to replace all the cut trees, and one of Oregon's greatest sources of natural beauty was shrinking.

Since the 1950s, forest workers have planted seedlings to replace some of the trees that are cut down each year.

In 1994 Oregon's forests gained protection from the Northwest Forest Plan. The plan set rules for the cutting of logs in Oregon. It stated that trees cannot be cut from national forests that are home to endangered species—plants and animals that are in danger of dying out entirely. But some biologists say that logging does not harm endangered species and their homes as much as was once thought.

Environmental activists continue to protest the logging of Oregon's old growth forests.

The future of logging and Oregon's forests and wildlife is uncertain.

While the state still relies heavily on lumber and wood products, jobs in other industries have increased. Over 60 percent of Oregonians work in service jobs. The national parks and preserved wilderness areas have created jobs in tourism, and the rise of high-tech industries has provided yet another major option for the workforce.

Oregon's natural beauty makes the state a popular vacation destination. This historic lighthouse on the Coquille River is found in Bullards Beach State Park, one of Oregon's many nature preserves.

Portland, Oregon's largest city, is home to about 527,000 people.

PEOPLE & ECONOMY

Diverse Resources

 lmost all of Oregon's 3.4 million people were born in the United States. Some Oregonians come from families of European descent who followed the Oregon Trail and settled in Oregon during the 1800s. Others trace their roots to Africa or Asia. Latinos make up about 8 percent of Oregon's people.

Only about 1 percent of the population is Native American. Some Indians live on one of Oregon's seven reservations. The largest Indian reservation is Warm Springs, on the eastern side of the Cascade Mountains.

A Native American boy dances at the Pendleton Round-Up, a rodeo in northeastern Oregon.

Oregon is the 10th largest state in the country, but it ranks 28th in number of people. Even in the state's cities, overcrowding has not been a problem. Most Oregonians live in the Willamette Valley, where the largest cities are located. These urban centers include Portland, Eugene, Salem (the capital), and Corvallis. Medford, in the southwest, is the largest city outside the valley.

Much of Oregon's cultural life takes place in Portland, the state's largest city. Portland has its own symphony orchestra and opera company. The Portland Art Museum, the Oregon Museum of Science and Industry, and the Oregon Historical Society draw thousands of visitors each year.

Some towns feature historical sites or American Indian art museums. The Seaside Museum in Seaside traces Oregon history with artifacts from 2,000 years ago to the present. Their displays cover Clatsop Indian history, early pioneers, recreation from Oregon's past, and railroad history in the area. The museum includes the historic Butterfield Cottage, which is a beach cottage of the 1912 era.

Portlanders build all-floral floats *(below)* for their city's Rose Festival, held each summer. The 17-day festival includes a Grand Floral Parade as well the Dragon Boat Race *(left)*.

Several towns around the state have annual events that celebrate life or history in their community.

Sports lovers find many exciting possibilities in Oregon. Hunters, fishers, skiers, boaters, hikers, and mountain climbers all enjoy the state's wilderness. Many top runners live in Eugene, which is often called the Track Capital of the World, because of its excellent running facilities. And NBA fans support the Portland Trail Blazers, a professional basketball team.

Contestants race for the finish line in the Mayor's Cup bicycle race in Portland.

Logging is still an important part of Oregon's economy.

Like the early settlers, many Oregonians still depend on natural resources such as trees and fertile soil for their livelihood. But compared to the early 1900s, only a few people are still loggers or farmers. More workers now make or sell products that are made from lumber or food crops.

Forests cover almost half of the state, and Oregon is one of the top producers of lumber in the country. Making wood products was the biggest industry in the state throughout much of the 1900s.

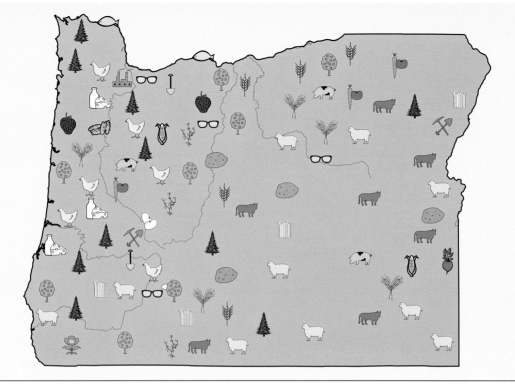

OREGON
Economic Map

The symbols on this map show where different economic activities take place in Oregon. The legend below explains what each symbol stands for.

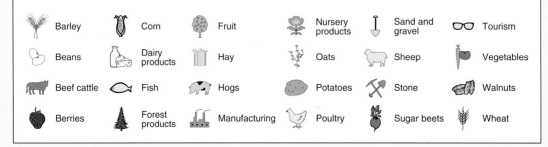

Barley	Corn	Fruit	Nursery products	Sand and gravel	Tourism
Beans	Dairy products	Hay	Oats	Sheep	Vegetables
Beef cattle	Fish	Hogs	Potatoes	Stone	Walnuts
Berries	Forest products	Manufacturing	Poultry	Sugar beets	Wheat

In the early 1980s, however, Oregon made less money from forest products because the demand for these goods dropped. Some mills closed because products could be made more cheaply elsewhere and many people lost their jobs. Finding new jobs for all the people who once worked in Oregon's lumber industry was a big challenge.

Manufacturing wood products has become Oregon's second leading industry. Some people in the lumber industry cut timber, plant trees, or make plywood, furniture, or mobile homes. Others work in sawmills or paper mills. Many of these items are shipped from Coos Bay, a busy coastal port, to places throughout the world.

Many of Oregon's products are shipped overseas from coastal ports.

In the 1990s, Oregon's economy improved. During the decade, a larger variety of jobs became available. The forestry products industry became stronger and high-tech industries became very successful. The state built new factories that make high-technology electronic products, such as computers and electrical equipment. Most of the

High-tech industries, such as computer production, have created many new jobs in Oregon.

people who work in the computer industry live and work just west of Portland, in an area nicknamed Silicon Forest—named after the material (silicon) used to make the small chips that store information in a computer.

Some factories in Oregon freeze, can, or freeze-dry food crops and then sell them to grocery stores throughout the country. Oregonians who work in food processing prepare many types of food for sale, including fruits, vegetables, meat, seafood, cheese, and sugar.

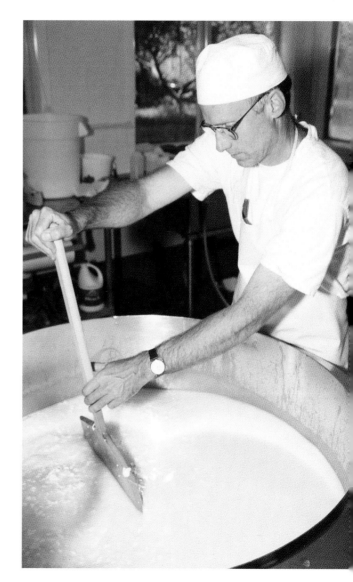

Many Oregonians work in the food-processing industry. This cheesemaker works on a small farm in rural Oregon.

Mild temperatures and plentiful rainfall make western Oregon a good place to grow a wide variety of crops. In the fertile valleys of the west, pears, apples, grapes, cherries, peaches, strawberries, beans, peas, and nuts thrive.

The Oregon grape *(left)*, Oregon's state flower, grows in the state's fertile western valleys. Several varieties of apples *(above)* grow there as well.

Oregon grows more hazelnuts and Christmas trees than any other state in the country.

Some farmers west of the Cascades raise poultry, hogs, and dairy cows, and larger herds of sheep and beef cattle roam the ranches of eastern Oregon. In this dry portion of the state, grains grow well. Wheat, for example, is the state's most valuable crop. Other grains raised in eastern Oregon include hay, barley, and oats. One of the few vegetables planted in the east is the potato.

Raising beef cattle is a major economic activity in eastern Oregon.

Oregon's rocky beaches, sand dunes, rugged mountains, clear lakes and rivers, and beautiful forests attract many visitors each year. In addition to its natural beauty, Oregon provides many kinds of entertainment in its large cities.

Tourism employs a lot of service workers in the state. Oregonians who work in hotels, restaurants, and airports provide services to make travelers more comfortable. Most of the growth in Oregon's job opportunities during the 1990s was in service jobs, especially jobs in tourism. Many other service jobs exist in Oregon. Engineers, bankers, and shopkeepers have jobs that help other people or businesses.

Many Oregonians work for the government. Public school and public hospital employees work for the government. The Forest Service, one of Oregon's largest government agencies, oversees the lumber industry and works to preserve Oregon's wilderness.

Visitors can find signs of prehistoric life at the John Day Fossil Beds in northeastern Oregon. Saber-toothed tigers, giant pigs, and three-toed horses are just a few of the creatures that once roamed this region.

THE ENVIRONMENT

Lumbering Forward

regon has some of the largest forests in the United States. But the rise of logging and other industries since the mid-1800s has threatened the future of Oregon's many trees.

In a state that depends on the lumber industry for money and jobs, protecting the forests is not easy. Some people in the state care most about keeping their jobs in lumbering. Others care more about preserving Oregon's forests. Still others are concerned about both the forests and the lumber industry.

Opposite page: Evergreen trees are a natural resource precious to both Oregon's nature-lovers and logging industry.

The government of Oregon has made many laws to protect forests in the state. In 1941 Oregon became the first state to require reforestation, or planting new trees, on all forest land after trees are cut down or after natural disasters, such as wildfires. The Forest Practices Act of 1971 requires even more reforestation after timber harvesting and outlines a program to prevent damage to woodlands, streams, and wildlife. The Oregon Department of Forestry teaches loggers to cut trees and build roads in ways that will do less harm to the environment.

Laws made in 1991 are even stricter. At least 200 seedlings must be planted per acre and maintained after planting. This is good both for the environment and the economy, and many public and private owners of forest land are eager to do more than the minimum required by law. Almost 80 million seedlings are planted every year. But it takes 60 to 80 years for the trees to mature. Only a small number of the forests left in Oregon contain old growth, trees that are between 200 and 1,200 years old.

These efforts have slowed the destruction of

Oregon's forests, but more could be done. Some Oregonians are asking the state's industries and residents to take further steps to protect their environment. These people, called environmentalists, would like to end the logging practice of **clear-cutting** (felling all the trees in an area). Clear-cutting wipes out the habitats of animals who live in the area.

After stripping entire hillsides bare *(below)*, forest workers plant seedlings *(left)*. But the young trees grow too slowly to completely repair the damage caused by clear-cutting.

With no trees left in clear-cut areas, certain kinds of fungi that grow around the roots of many trees die. These small life-forms use the live trees for their source of energy. In turn, the fungi help the

trees absorb water and nutrients. Without the fungi, trees planted in clear-cut areas may not survive. The practice of thinning forests, selecting only some trees for cutting rather than completely clearing an area, helps protect all the wild plants and animals that live in the forests.

As the old growth forests disappear, so do some kinds of wildlife that depend on them for habitats. For example, the spotted owl can live only in the thick, dark, older forests. In the early 1990s, the spotted owl was declared threatened. The U.S. Fish and Wildlife Service ordered logging to be stopped in several old growth forests to protect the owls' habitat.

Oregonians want to balance the benefits of harvesting the forests for timber with

Spotted owl

protecting the water, wildlife, and soil of the forests. In 1993 a "timber summit," arranged by President Bill Clinton, was held in Oregon. A compromise was reached that allowed some logging but also provided money to train loggers for new jobs. The Forest Service has estimated that in the year 2000, recreation, hunting, and fishing in the National Forests created more jobs and contributed more money to the nation's economy than logging did.

The debate continues and Oregonians work toward finding a balance. As the "clean" high-tech and tourism industries offer jobs not dependent on using up natural resources, the future of Oregon's forests looks brighter.

Oregonians are working together to manage their state's forests carefully.

ALL ABOUT OREGON

Fun Facts

In 1971 Oregon became the first state to require that all beverage cans and bottles be returnable.

The Oregon Trail was the longest overland route traveled by pioneers moving west. Starting in Missouri and ending in Oregon's Willamette Valley, the trail stretched across 2,000 miles of prairie, mountains, and desert. The difficult journey took four to six months by covered wagon.

Some of the fir trees in Oregon's forests are more than 1,000 years old. They can measure over 250 feet tall—that's almost as high as the Statue of Liberty!

Mill Ends Park in Portland, Oregon, is the smallest official park in the world. Just two feet across, it was created on Saint Patrick's Day in 1948 as a home for leprechauns and as a snail-racing site. It was made a city park in 1976.

Recyclables

The name Oregon may have come from the name French people gave the Columbia River. They called this waterway Ouragan, which means "hurricane," probably because of the strong rainstorms that blow in from the sea and travel up the river.

Western Oregon gets so much rain that the people who live there have been nick-named Webfoots. Folklore says that babies in the region are born with webs between their toes so they can paddle, like ducks, across wet land.

Hells Canyon in northeastern Oregon is the deepest river-carved gorge in North America. The canyon has an average depth of 5,500 feet and goes down as far as about 8,000 feet in some places. Hells Canyon is part of the 652,500-acre Hells Canyon National Recreation Area.

STATE SONG

Oregonians held a contest to choose a state song in 1920, and "Oregon, My Oregon" was the winner. The song was officially adopted in 1927.

OREGON, MY OREGON

Words by J. A. Buchanan; music by Henry B. Murtagh

You can hear "Oregon, My Oregon" by visiting this website:
<http://www.50states.com/songs/oregon.htm>

AN OREGON RECIPE

Oregon produces about 99 percent of the hazelnuts, also called filberts, in the United States. Young hazel trees were first brought to Oregon from the Loire Valley, a region in France. The round nut's sweet chewiness makes it a good addition to many kinds of recipes—sweet or not.

HAZELNUT CHOCOLATE CAKE

1 (18.25-ounce) box chocolate cake mix
1 (3-ounce) box instant chocolate pudding mix
1 teaspoon vanilla extract
¼ cup water

3 cups heavy whipping cream
1½ cup semisweet chocolate chips
1 cup chopped hazelnuts
12 whole hazelnuts

1. Prepare cake mix batter according to instructions on box. Add pudding mix, vanilla, and ¼ cup water. Divide batter into 3 greased 9-inch round cake pans. With an adult's help, bake 18–22 minutes. Set aside to cool.
2. With an adult's help, melt chocolate chips in double-boiler. Slowly stir in ¼ cup whipping cream. Cool.
3. Beat ¾ cup whipping cream until soft peaks form. Stir into cooled chocolate mixture. Stir in ½ cup of chopped hazelnuts. Chill for 30 minutes.
4. Beat remaining 2 cups whipping cream until soft peaks form. Add the remaining ½ cup chopped hazelnuts. Chill untill ready to frost cake.
5. Spread half of chilled chocolate mixture on first cake layer. Add second cake layer. Spread the other half of the chocolate on cake. Top with last cake layer. Frost the entire cake with hazelnut whipped cream.
6. Place 12 whole hazelnuts around the top edge for decoration. Keep cake refrigerated.

HISTORICAL TIMELINE

10,000 B.C. Indians live at Fort Rock Caves in Oregon.

5000 B.C. Mount Mazama erupts, erasing signs of life at Fort Rock.

A.D. 1792 Robert Gray is the first white person to sail into the Columbia River.

1805 The Lewis and Clark expedition reaches Oregon by land.

1821 John McLoughlin comes to Oregon to head the Hudson's Bay Company.

1843 The first large group of immigrants comes to Oregon in covered wagons.

1846 The United States and Britain split up the Oregon Country.

1859 Oregon joins the Union as the 33rd state on February 14.

1877 Chief Joseph and the Nez Perce are defeated by the U.S. Army in the Nez Perce War.

1883 The Northern Pacific Railroad opens. Oregonians send lumber to the East Coast faster than ever before.

1888 Portland's population reaches 60,000, making it the largest community in the Pacific Northwest.

1902 Oregon becomes the third state to adopt the initiative and referendum, procedures that allow voters a more active role in lawmaking.

1912 Oregon becomes the sixth state to give women the right to vote.

1937 Bonneville Dam is completed, making it possible for large ships to travel 200 miles up the Columbia River.

1941 Oregon is the first state to require reforestation.

1970 The Portland Trail Blazers, a professional basketball team, begin competing.

1971 The Forest Practices Act is passed to help preserve Oregon's wilderness areas. A "bottle bill" is signed in Oregon, prohibiting nonreturnable beverage bottles.

1991 The first woman governor of Oregon, Barbara Roberts, takes office.

1993 President Bill Clinton holds a "timber summit" in Oregon.

2002 Smoking is outlawed in Oregon's workplaces.

OUTSTANDING OREGONIANS

John Jacob Astor

John Jacob Astor (1763–1848) was a fur trader who set up the Pacific Fur Company in 1810 to compete with the British fur trade in the Oregon Country. The following year, Astor founded the town of Astoria, the first permanent settlement in Oregon.

Carl Barks (1901–2000) was a cartoonist originally from Merrill, Oregon. Barks illustrated the Walt Disney cartoon "Donald Duck." In 1947 he created the character Uncle Scrooge McDuck to add to the comic.

Beverly Cleary

Beverly Cleary (born 1916), who grew up in McMinnville, Oregon, has written many books for children. She is best known for her books about the adventures of Henry Huggins and Ramona Quimby, who live in a suburb of Portland.

Ann Curry (born 1956) is a television news reporter. She began her career at the Medford, Oregon, television station KTVL in 1978. In 1990 she joined NBC News and has been the news anchor for NBC's *Today Show* since 1997. Curry, who grew up in southern Oregon, has received the NAACP Award for Excellence in Reporting and won the Golden Mike award four times.

David Douglas

David Douglas (1798–1834) was a Scottish explorer and botanist. He traveled through California, Oregon, and British Columbia and described the plants he found. The Douglas fir, Oregon's state tree, is named after him.

Abigail Jane Scott Duniway

Abigail Jane Scott Duniway (1834–1915) was one of the first women in the United States to fight for women's rights. After her husband became an invalid, she supported him and her family of six children by running a hat shop in Albany, Oregon. Her work made her aware of laws that treated men and women unequally, and she began to demand fair treatment for women. Her efforts helped women gain the right to vote in three states—Oregon, Washington, and Idaho.

Matt Groening

Matt Groening (born 1954) is the creator of *The Simpsons*, the longest-running prime-time animated show on television. Born in Portland, Groening first gained attention with his comic strip, *Life in Hell.* The characters in *The Simpsons* were named after members of Groening's own family, except for Bart, which is an anagram (has the same letters) of brat.

Keintpoos

Keintpoos (died 1873), known as Captain Jack, led a group of Modoc Indians during the 1860s. Together they fought to maintain their traditional way of life rather than live on a reservation. The U.S. Army eventually captured Keintpoos, and he was tried, found guilty, and executed on October 3, 1873.

Ken Kesey

Ken Kesey (1935–2001) was a writer who grew up on a Springfield, Oregon, farm. His first novel, *One Flew over the Cuckoo's Nest*, published in 1962, was a best-seller and was turned into a film. His second novel, *Sometimes a Great Notion*, tells the story of an Oregonian logging family. Kesey lived on a farm in Pleasant Hill, Oregon, from 1965 until his death.

Philip H. Knight

Philip H. Knight (born 1938), a native of Portland, was one of two businessmen who founded Nike, Inc., a sports-gear company named after the Greek goddess of victory. At first called Blue Ribbon Sports, Nike got its start in 1964, when Knight began selling running shoes from his father's basement. In 2000 the Beaverton, Oregon, company earned $9.5 billion.

Evelyn Sibley Lampman (1907–1980) was born in Dallas, Oregon, and died in Portland. She wrote several books for children, including *The City under the Back Steps, Halfbreed,* and *Cayuse Coyote.* She used the pen name Lynn Bronson on some of her books.

Ursula K. Le Guin

Ursula K. Le Guin (born 1929) is a writer of science fiction and fantasy tales. *The Tombs of Atuan,* the second book in her Earthsea series for children, was a Newbery Honor Book. She also writes poetry and essays. Le Guin lives in Portland, Oregon.

Thomas Lawson McCall (1913–1983) served as governor of Oregon from 1967 to 1975. He supported environmental laws, cleaned up Oregon's rivers, and limited building along the coast of Oregon. During McCall's term in office, Oregon passed the first state law in the country requiring beverage cans and bottles to be returnable.

John McLoughlin

John McLoughlin (1784–1857) was a Canadian who became known as the Father of Oregon. As a fur trader, McLoughlin headed the Hudson's Bay Company and helped build Fort Vancouver in 1825. He encouraged many people to settle in the Oregon Country.

Wayne L. Morse

Wayne L. Morse (1900–1974) represented Oregon as a U.S. senator from 1945 to 1969. Committed to examining facts and policies carefully, Morse was an advocate of civil rights and, in the 1960s, an outspoken critic of the Vietnam War.

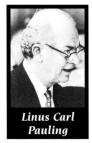

Linus Carl Pauling

Linus Carl Pauling (1901–1994) was a chemist and physicist from Portland. In 1954 he won a Nobel Prize in chemistry for discoveries that helped doctors solve medical problems. Eight years later—in 1962—he won a Nobel Peace Prize for the work he had done to stop the testing of nuclear weapons. Such testing posed a serious health threat to millions of people throughout the world.

Ahmad Rashad (born 1949), who originally came from Portland, played college football at the University of Oregon where he was a two-time All-American. He then played professional football from 1972 to 1982, and was a four-time Pro Bowl selection for the Minnesota Vikings. He is an Emmy Award-winning sportscaster for NBC.

Ahmad Rashad

Barbara Roberts (born 1936) is a fourth-generation Oregonian, born in Corvallis, who became Oregon's first woman governor in 1991. Roberts began her career in politics working for the rights of handicapped children. She served as governor until 1995 and strongly supported public education, human rights, and helping the environment.

Barbara Roberts

Alberto Salazar (born 1958), a long-distance runner, won the New York City Marathon three times and the Boston Marathon once. Born in Cuba, Salazar trained as a runner and lives in Eugene, Oregon. In 1994 he won the Comrades Marathon, a 53-mile race in South Africa. He was inducted into the National Distance Running Hall of Fame in 2000.

Mary Decker Slaney

Mary Decker Slaney (born 1958) is a professional middle-distance runner who lives in Eugene, Oregon. She has set many American and world track records and competed in the 1984, 1988, and 1996 Olympics. At the end of the twentieth century she was named one of the top 100 female athletes by *Sports Illustrated* magazine.

John Yeon (1910–1994), an architect, is from Portland. He taught himself much of what he knows. He is especially noted for using landscape to make his buildings more attractive.

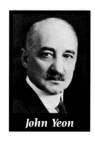

John Yeon

FACTS-AT-A-GLANCE

Nickname: Beaver State

Song: "Oregon, My Oregon"

Motto: *Alis Volat Propiis* (She Flies with Her Own Wings)

Flower: Oregon grape

Tree: Douglas fir

Bird: western meadowlark

Animal: American beaver

Fish: Chinook salmon

Nut: hazelnut

Mushroom: Pacific golden chanterelle

Date and ranking of statehood: February 14, 1859, the 33rd state

Capital: Salem

Area: 96,002 square miles

Rank in area, nationwide: 10th

Average January temperature: 32° F

Average July temperature: 66° F

Oregon adopted its state flag in 1925. The shield from the state seal, in gold, is in the center of one side of the blue flag. There are 33 stars around the shield, because Oregon became the 33rd state in 1859, the date which is written under the shield. A beaver is shown on the other side. Oregon is the only state with a different pattern on the reverse side of its flag.

POPULATION GROWTH

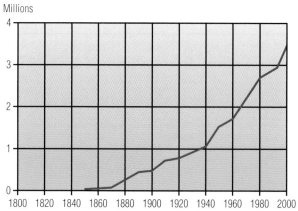

Millions

This chart shows how Oregon's population has grown from 1850 to 2000.

The state seal bears a shield with a ribbon reading "The Union." Atop the shield is an American Eagle, and surrounding it are 33 stars. Under the shield's ribbon, wheat, a plow, and a pickax represent miners and farmers. Above, a covered wagon represents the pioneers. Oregon's mountains and forests are set against the rays of the sun over the Pacific Ocean. A British ship departs while an American ship arrives.

Population: 3,421,399 (2000 census)

Rank in population, nationwide: 28th

Major cities and populations: (2000 census) Portland (526,986), Eugene (137,893), Salem (119,040), Gresham (90,205), Beaverton (76,129), Hillsboro (70,186)

U.S. senators: 2

U.S. representatives: 5

Electoral votes: 7

Natural resources: clay, coal, copper, gemstones, gold, gravel, lead, limestone, natural gas, nickel, pumice, sand, silver, soil, talc, timber, water

Agricultural products: apples, barley, beef cattle, berries, cherries, Christmas trees, dairy cows, flower bulbs, grapes, grass seeds, hay, hazelnuts, hogs, milk, oats, peaches, pears, peppermint oil, potatoes, poultry, sheep, timber, vegetables, wheat

Fishing industry: crab, shrimp, tuna, whiting

Manufactured goods: computers, electrical equipment, frozen fruits and vegetables, lumber and wood products, machinery, metals, paper products, scientific instruments

WHERE OREGONIANS WORK

Services—63 percent (services includes jobs in trade; community, social, and personal services; finance, insurance, and real estate; transportation, communication, and utilities)

Manufacturing—13 percent

Government—13 percent

Construction—6 percent

Agriculture—5 percent

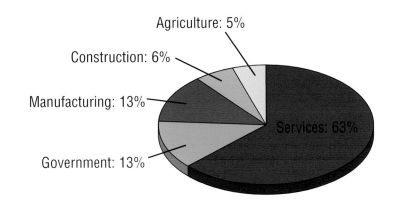

Agriculture: 5%

Construction: 6%

Manufacturing: 13%

Government: 13%

Services: 63%

GROSS STATE PRODUCT

Services—59 percent

Manufacturing—21 percent

Government—11 percent

Construction—6 percent

Agriculture—3 percent

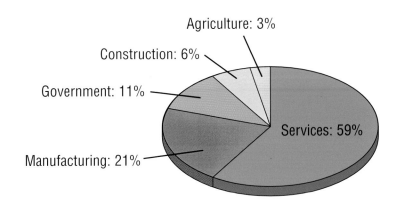

Agriculture: 3%

Construction: 6%

Government: 11%

Manufacturing: 21%

Services: 59%

OREGON WILDLIFE

Mammals: beaver, bighorn sheep, black bear, deer, elk, fox, mountain goat, pronghorn antelope, river otter, sea lion, sea otter, seals, whales

Birds: brown pelican, cormorant, cranes, ducks, eagles, great blue heron, osprey, owls, puffin, tern, western meadowlark

Reptiles: green sea turtle, leatherback sea turtle, lizards, rattlesnake

Fish: bass, clams, cod, halibut, herring, perch, salmon, shrimp, sole, squid, sturgeon, trout, tuna

Trees: alder, ash, cedar, cottonwood, firs, hemlock, juniper, maple, pines, spruce, willow

Wild plants: azaleas, buckbrush, camas lily, Indian paintbrush, grasses, laurels, Oregon grape, red huckleberry, sagebrush

Beavers make their homes in Oregon's many lakes and rivers.

PLACES TO VISIT

Astoria's Waterfront, northwestern Oregon

Astoria, founded in 1811, was once the Salmon Canning Capital of the World. Astoria is still a fishing town and its working waterfront is a tourist destination. A riverfront walk connects docked fishing boats with museums and with packinghouses.

Bonneville Dam, on the Columbia River

This enormous dam controls flooding and produces electricity along the Columbia River. Salmon swim upstream by leaping up special fish ladders. A visitor center is open to the public.

Columbia River Gorge National Scenic Area, northern Oregon

You can view the 8-mile-long gorge by hiking along the shore or from a tour boat. The USDA Forest Service manages this area, which covers more than 15.5 million acres.

Crater Lake National Park, near Fort Klamath

This is one of Oregon's most spectacular areas. Crater Lake was formed from the mouth of a collapsed volcano more than 6,500 years ago. The lake, famous for its crystal blue waters, is the deepest lake in the United States.

End of the Oregon Trail Interpretive Center, Oregon City

The huge interpretive center tells the story of the early pioneers who traveled 2,000 dangerous miles across the Oregon Trail to start new lives in the Pacific Northwest. In addition to the indoor theaters and exhibit hall, an outdoor hands-on area gives visitors a physical sense of what life was like for children of the period.

John Day Fossil Beds National Monument, near John Day
Saber-toothed tiger bones are among the many fossils of plants and animals dating back 55 million years that have been found in the John Day River Basin. The site includes the Painted Hills, a geological wonder whose colored stripes are caused by layers of 40-million-year-old volcanic ash deposits.

Mount Hood, northwestern Oregon
This beautiful snow-capped peak (and dormant volcano) is the highest point in Oregon. It is surrounded by a national forest where you can camp, hike, snowboard, and enjoy the wilderness.

Oregon Coast Aquarium, Newport
View jellyfish, whales, sea otters and many other types of marine life at inside and outside displays. In the Passages of the Deep exhibit, visitors walk through clear tubes above the ocean floor.

Oregon Dunes National Recreation Area, western Oregon
This area offers some of the West Coast's best beach-oriented recreation. Hike through sand dunes that rise over 500 feet high.

Oregon Museum of Science and Industry, Portland
Science enthusiasts can visit a planetarium and explore a real Navy submarine here. There are over 100 interactive exhibits to choose from. Other exhibits include an earthquake room, a chicken hatchery, and a hands-on space station.

Silver Falls State Park, western Oregon
At Oregon's largest state park, there are miles of hiking trails that lead through forests and past ten waterfalls. You can walk behind many of the falls.

ANNUAL EVENTS

Oregon Shakespeare Festival, Ashland—*February–November*

Loyalty Days, Newport—*May*

Pioneer Day, Jacksonville—*June*

Portland Rose Festival—*May–June*

Cannon Beach Sand Castle Contest—*July*

Dory Days Parade and Dory Boat Race, Pacific City—*July*

World Championship Timber Carnival, Albany—*July*

Hood to Coast Relay Race, Mount Hood to Seaside—*August*

Homowo (West African Thanksgiving) Festival, Portland—*August*

Pendleton Roundup and Happy Canyon Pageant, Pendelton—*September*

Fall International Kite Festival, Lincoln City—*September*

Kraut and Sausage Feed and Bazaar, Verboort—*November*

Dia de Nuestra Señora de Guadalupe (Feast Day of the Virgin of Guadalupe), Medford—*December*

Festival of Trees, Newport—*December*

LEARN MORE ABOUT OREGON

BOOKS

General

Fradin, Dennis, and Judith Bloom Fradin. *Oregon.* Chicago: Children's Press. 1995.

Ingram, Scott. *Oregon.* New York: Children's Press, 2000. For older readers.

Wills, Charles. *A Historical Album of Oregon.* Brookfield, CT: Millbrook Press, 1995.

Special Interest

Cleary, Beverly. *A Girl from Yamhill.* New York: Avon Books, 1999. The autobiography of the author of the Ramona Quimby and Henry Huggins books. Beverly Cleary grew up in Oregon during the Great Depression. Readers will enjoy seeing the connection between the author's life and some of the episodes that show up in her books. For older readers.

Littlefield, Holly. *Children of the Trail West.* Minneapolis: Carolrhoda Books, Inc., 1999. Thousands of children and their families traveled on the Oregon Trail in the 1800s. Full of historical photos, this book shows what it was like to cross prairies and mountains in a wagon.

Marsh, Carole. *Oregon History!: Surprising Secrets about Our State's Founding Mothers, Father, and Kids!* Peachtree City, GA: Gallopade, 1996. This book answers the question: Why should kids care about Oregon's history?

Rapp, Valerie. *Life in an Old Growth Forest.* Minneapolis: Lerner Publications Company, 2003. Learn about the animals and plants that live in the ancient forests of the western United States, including Oregon's Willamette Forest. For older readers.

Fiction

Cleary, Beverly. *Ramona and Her Father.* New York: Morrow, 1977. Ramona Quimby is an adventurous second-grader who lives with her loving, but struggling, family in a suburb of Portland. In this book, Ramona must deal with the ups and downs of modern family life.

Lampman, Evelyn Sibley. *The Shy Stegosaurus of Cricket Creek.* 1955. Reprint, Keller, TX: Purple House Press, 2001. Twins Joey and Joan find George, a living dinosaur, while hunting in the desert for fossils. Lighthearted adventure follows as George tries to help his friends raise money for their mother's ranch.

Marsh, Carole. *Chill Out!: Scary Oregon Stories Based on Frightening Oregon.* Peachtree City, GA: Gallopade, 1992. Pirates, ghosts, and bloody rooms haunt these fictional stories set in Oregon.

Van Leeuwen, Jean. *Bound for Oregon.* New York: Puffin Books, 1996. Nine-year-old Mary Ellen tells the story of life with her family as they travel the Oregon Trail, starting from Arkansas with only 40 pounds of food and two spare wagon wheels.

WEBSITES

Oregon.gov
<http://www.oregon.gov>
The state's official website, Oregon.gov is the state's central web portal. This site is organized by themes, including Oregon facts, business, education, tourism, and government. A Kids Only section has links to other useful sites.

Travel Oregon Online
<http://www.traveloregon.com>
Sponsored by the Oregon Tourism Commission, this site lists fourteen "must see sights" in the state. It includes an events calendar and provides information needed to plan a vacation, from outlining regional attractions to helping find lodging.

Oregon*Live*.com
<http://www.oregonlive.com>
The online version of *The Oregonian*, Portland's daily newspaper, Oregon*Live*.com features news, sports, entertainment calendars, webcasts, chat rooms, and more. The site's home page is updated three times daily with the latest breaking news.

Oregon Coast Aquarium
<http://www.aquarium.org/>
This aquarium is the home of Keiko the orca, star of the movie *Free Willy*. Tour the many exhibits or link to the live Keiko cam.

PRONUNCIATION GUIDE

Bonneville (BAHN-uh-vihl)

Cayuse (KY-yoos)

Chinook (SHUH-NOOK)

Columbia Plateau (kuh-LUHM-bee-uh pla-TOH)

Deschutes (dih-SHOOTS)

Eugene (yoo-JEEN)

McLoughlin (muh-KLAWF-luhn)

Nez Perce (NEZ PURS)

Paiute (PIE-yoot)

Rogue (ROHG)

Umpqua (UHMP-kwaw)

Vancouver (van-KOO-vur)

Willamette (wuh-LAM-uht)

Oregon draws lovers of outdoor activity from near and far. Both residents and tourists enjoy kayaking in the Dechutes River at Drake Park near Bend, Oregon.

GLOSSARY

archaeologist: a person who studies ancient times and places by digging up what is left of their cities, buildings, tombs, and other remains

canyon: a narrow valley that has steep, rocky cliffs on its sides

clear-cutting: a method of cutting forests that removes all the trees in an area

desert: an area of land that receives only about 10 inches or less of rain or snow a year. Some deserts are mountainous; others are expanses of rock, sand, or salt flats

hydropower: the electricity produced by using water power; also called hydroelectric power

immigrant: a person who moves into a foreign country and settles there

irrigation: watering land by directing water through canals, ditches, pipes, or sprinklers

lava: hot, melted rock that erupts from a volcano or from cracks in the earth's surface and hardens as it cools

missionary: a person sent out by a religious group to spread its beliefs to other people

plateau: a large, relatively flat area that stands above the surrounding land

reservation: public land set aside by the government to be used by Native Americans

treaty: an agreement between two or more groups, usually having to do with peace or trade

INDEX

PHOTO ACKNOWLEDGMENTS

© Buddy Mays/Travel Stock, pp. 2–3, 6, 54, 80; © Pat O'Hara/CORBIS, p. 3 (right); © Kitty Kohout/Root Resources, p. 4, 7, 18 (detail), 41 (detail), 55; © Ron Bell/Presentationmaps.com, pp. 8, 9, 46; © Emily Slowinski, p. 10; Oregon State Parks, pp. 11, 12; © Jan G. Bannon/Root Resources, pp. 13, 50 (right); © Larry Schaefer/Root Resources, p. 15; USDA Forest Service, pp. 16, 18, 53, 57 (both), 59; © Stan Osolinski/Root Resources, p. 17; © James Blank /Root Resources, p. 19; Royal Ontario Museum, Department of Ethnology, Toronto, Canada, p. 20; Oregon Historical Society, pp. 21 (neg. # 4466), 23, 27 (neg. #5231), 28, 33 (neg. #144), 34 (neg. # 67701), 35, 37 (neg. #085015), 66 (second from bottom and bottom, negs. #19683 and #4599), 68 (second from top, neg. #251), 68 (bottom, neg. #78523), 69 (bottom, neg. #CN 018349); University of Minnesota, p. 22; Bryan Peterson/Legislative Media Services, p. 24; © Bettmann/CORBIS, pp. 29; Smithsonian Institution National Anthropological Archives, Bureau of American Ethnology Collection, pp. 30 (neg. #2906), 67 (second from top, neg. #430132); Library of Congress, pp. 32, 68 (second from bottom); © Gary Braasch/CORBIS, pp. 36; AP/Wide World Photos, pp. 38, 48; Commander Bruce Hillard/National Oceanographic and Atmospheric Administration, p. 39; © Steve Vidler/SuperStock, p. 40; Oregon Tourism Division, p. 41; Portland Rose Festival Association, p. 43 (both); © Mount Burns, pp. 44, 47; Deschutes National Forest, p. 45; © Craig Lovell/CORBIS, pp. 49; © Kathleen Marie Manke, p. 50 (left); © Walter Gorham, p. 51; © Kenneth W. Fink/Root Resources, p. 58; Department of Environmental Quality, p. 60; Jack Lindstrom, p. 61; New York Public Library, p. 66 (top); Margaret Miller/William Morrow & Co., p. 66 (second from top); Photofest, pp. 67 (top and second from bottom), 68 (top); Nike, Inc., p. 67 (bottom); Minnesota Vikings, p. 69 (top); Oregon State Archives, p. 69 (second from top); © Wally McNamee/CORBIS, p. 69 (second from bottom); Jean Matheny, p. 70 (top); © Allen G. Nelson/Root Resource, p. 73.

Front Cover (left): © Richard Cummins/CORBIS
Front Cover (right): © Philip James Corwin/CORBIS